T0037730

IN THE DAYS THAT FOLLOWED

IN THE DAYS THAT FOLLOWED

Kevin Goodan

Alice James Books
New Gloucester, Maine
alicejamesbooks.org

Printed in the United States

10 9 8 7 6 5 4 3 2 1

Alice James Books are published by Alice James Poetry Cooperative, Inc.

Alice James Books
Auburn Hall
60 Pineland Drive, Suite 206
New Gloucester, ME 04260
www.alicejamesbooks.org

Library of Congress Cataloging-in-Publication Data

Names: Goodan, Kevin, 1969- author.
Title: In the days that followed / Kevin Goodan.
Description: New Gloucester, Maine : Alice James Books, 2024.
Identifiers: LCCN 2023053358 (print) | LCCN 2023053359 (ebook) | ISBN 9781949944617 (trade paperback) | ISBN 9781949944334 (epub)
Subjects: LCGFT: Poetry.
Classification: LCC PS3607.O563 I48 2024 (print) | LCC PS3607.O563 (ebook) | DDC 811/.6--dc23/eng/20231116
LC record available at https://lccn.loc.gov/2023053358
LC ebook record available at https://lccn.loc.gov/2023053359

Alice James Books gratefully acknowledges support from individual donors, private foundations, and the National Endowment for the Arts.

Cover image: “Sparrow,” oil on canvas, 30 x 40 cm © 2021 Javier Arean.
www.javierarean.com

CONTENTS

For those who live with us in
a dimension we are not yet
allowed to see

SHALL I INVOKE?

The iris opens,
Snags fall on water,
A bee breaks down a flower
With its body of lead
That melts in the sun
That stabs its blades
When the scorching is silent.
The wheat-brush buckles
And the fur of the animals
Carries forth the flame
To where a hand opens
And a match appears,
Blue rifles at the ready—
Ah, to torch, to walk from
What we once loved
And called home.

THERE ARE THINGS I KNOW

Called by other names:
Hunker and hooch,
Graupel and dust, angel lust,
A serious nimbus above
The ur-tongue larks sing
As day opens to a violence,
Rotations of rain, the urgency
Of the agency of what we name
The other: rust-buckled combine
In the muck of a field,
No quail to avail for their burble
In the brush, the flat report
Of a blast in the slough as we
Traverse the uneven ground
Of the naming.

POPCORN CLOUDS BRIGHTER THAN THE HOUR,
A thin blue beyond where no one lives
That I dream, though they live surely
As purgations of form, making certain
Everyone is named that wants to be,
Some carrying the knives and hammers
Of their going, clasped always in the
Left hand of their shining—
You who are purity, breathe with me
Now as you stand correcting my entries,
Carry me forward, for I am without means,
You who guard the barrier, children
Of the passageway, children of the river.

WHAT MORE BELONGS TO US?

This, too, is complicated
Because we are living
Though daisies wither
In late-July sun, and clover
Blooms are all buzz and
Harbor, now that the night
Mist vanishes, and the spray-
Plane makes a low pass
On fields beyond my eyes
And banks the rucks
Of the ungodded hour
Before the mid-dawn stifle
Where even your voice
Sweats into silence,
And now the straight-line
Wind bringing strange
Sadness to the blood
Like moans from a house
We've never lived in,
Some vestigial wraith
That owns our hearts,
That bleeds out
The poor souls of Heaven.

BASIL BLOOMING RANCID IN THE SUN

As bees master clover
And the utility of serviceberry,
The truth of chokecherry,
Of huckleberry blooding the hand
As hummingbirds bicker and veer
As quail come in the numbers
Of God, and the constant hawk
Taking the needed. I am
In the calm where moths reside
As thorns pluck wires of the screens
In a music of no one, and I'm witnessing
That a word is a moment, an increment
To be held of the passing earth
Like calls of anywhere through a stand
Of dark trees, of anywhere.

AND WHAT'S TO BE DONE WITH BRIGHTNESS?

Ah, the winter-bells tolling in the blood
Where sky leaches down its slush,
A dusting for the eyes when the abstract
Becomes a taste on the tongue.
Who are we that we should yearn for such
Higher music. Like geese calling
Through the first snow in our flesh—
Winter-bell, winter-bell, feel the chill
Of the inward tolling, of a lesser world.

SOME SENSE OF MORNING ARRIVAL

On the rain-sprailed window
The way coldness translates
A body, a phrase that is granted
And cannot be lived up to:
Know thy wings. Outside,
Green nubs of wheat thrusting
Through November—
Wonky barn, silo, tendrils
Of pine smoke, oh radials
Of light, where our eyes are
No different than weather,
Where I say: *Is it you I'm waiting for?*

NO DEER, BUT TRACKS OF THEM,
Flattened weeds of their sleeping—
Bright sheens of hoar
Where the sun burns through
And will not abate in the blear
That December throws
The blued hatchings of a limited sky—
Will you not grant the vision, the words,
Your words? The hidden expense
Of prayer is time. I want to live
To know answers the rose,
Garlanded with frost, knows.
For in the blood of Joseph
I have seen you, have entered
Into the communion that weeping is.
For the saddest moments are in the watching
And the watching of dream
Where I move through the silvered air
Into the gray zones a wind cannot touch.

WHAT WILL BE RELINQUISHED?

Whose small hand will you let slip
From yours before it is time?
8:13 am, the fields are greening
where dark birds gather—
fusty hour, rabbit hour, what
flees a shadow but holds a harm,
hawk, hawk's beak, hawk's bane,
the give, the granted, the want
as you live. The catch it all,
the hold it all, the breathe it all
home.

AND SO, WE TURN FROM THE WINDOW

To feel the bells within us
Tolling in a tower where it's
Almost light. Doves cluster
The telephone wires along a field
Where an old man parks
The red pickup and leads the boy
Through the ripe stalks down
Into the steam of the river
Where beasts rise from the darkness
Of the tolling to drink the shallows
Where a fire has burned, is burning
In small jets of flame, where
A book has been opened, is waiting.

ASH WILL FIND YOU

And you will breathe it in
And it will be as though
You have awakened
Under the weight of other
Bodies, and you will
Know them, for they were
The ones burning
In your dreams.

OWL PELLETS ON THE PITCH OF THE ROOF.
Robins feeding in snow where sins
Of the mother replay, and when I slit
The lamb's throat, God does not look.
What noise snow brings to the caking
Of these hands, hymns of the shadow
Open at my feet as I strip and flense
And carve and wipe a brow with smear
As a halo emerges above the sun's rising,
As snow sifts a dissected heart.

WHEN A FIST-SIZED GOD SMACKS THE WINDOW

It leaves a mark: snot and blood. Rain does
To us what the rain does, hard. And yet
We thrive at the borders where the voice
Of you quails, is snatched, and we keep
Crossing the river to bathe in the waters
Of the unsayable. From the air, one sees
What could not be held. Each moment is
A shadow of them and the night sky grows
Cold and dense with presence, those beings
Who are born without mouths and for a time
Are perfect, and unawake.

FROM ETERNAL SOUNDS OF DREAM I WAKE,
Tinnitus of hearing a world,
Frost cusping green grass, frost on tin,
The leafy clots of willow, of poplar,
A windlessness that is darkness
From the west, temporary bounty,
And it happens now when nothing remains
But starling and starling, the quadrants
Of a life that moves with weather,
Where I write with a pistol aimed
Always at the vagueness that invades my mind
Where the vertigoes I know require
Flesh, a bit of blood on the saw,
The guts of a day displayed to other
Judgments, where we slice
The surface tension of any heart
And open its rooms to the furnace
Of this single hour.

WHAT IS THE WEIGHT OF GONE?

Of all fires, this one.
We write toward a beauty
Where words cannot exist.
Here, it's March, the deer
Bed down in a subsidence
Of wind. The last cuff
Of slush crumples into green.
In the glacial seep of the dream
I've set words on the long sill
To force them in the heat.

THIS BEING WHAT MARCH HAS MEANT—
Smell of night-snow on grass
That's greened, a feral crocus
Thrusting its stubborn nub
To the schreep of mongrel birds
That linger through the pour
As fields rupture into flood,
Salvo after salvo of storm,
A vital hail blustered with thunder,
Here, then far, the outhouse
Slushed, canted toward slough,
The galvanized sheet metal whomping
The mud, pausing an endless
Monologuing mind that hears
Storm-dark wood once more,
A clarity exhaustion brings
Where shades of past harms
Enter the near distance
All tensile and bright—
What sequence saved us?
Blue slash through the air?
As we enter the diurnal murk,
A yardlight to pray from,
And what comes upon us
In the field's constant splay
Is not the hope we'd hoped for,
Not that, but what takes root
In each small chest, constricts
And bursts into bloom unnamed.

THE NIBS OF WEEDS THAT SCRIBBLE THE WEATHER,
Electric crickets of a northern dawn
A Cessna arcs through, stalls, as larks
On power poles try stitching the moment
Together. Soon, there will be storms,
Scent of hay tossed before rain.
We look up from the woodpile,
The lanky chunks of pine we scrounged
Waiting for the pistons to charge.
The larks sing faster in the elongations
Of light, as the plane dips and I feel
The gears of time beginning to mesh.
Or will the everyday gods intervene?
Yellowjackets preen and glint
And we talk about how there is
No true north, only the wandering
Polarities that keep us to this earth.

WHEN I LOOK BACK, THE BLACKBIRD HAS RISEN

In its cup of sound, the hornet trap glistens
With the curved forms of the taken,
The scent of someone being here before,
Someone on the way of peril, through
The stubble of Endicott, across the loess,
Where we listen for love's diminishment.
Wind through a brawl of lilac
Where a farm used to be, where even weeds
Yearn and fail to flower, and I see
In the dust faint marks that are a code
I have no choice but to follow.

OH, THE MURMURATIONS

That have swarmed me,
Tinge of the river,
Tinge of the river,
Crenellations that are
The light's way
Of saying you do not
Belong to this—
The days out, the long days
Back, with loneliness
At the ports of entry
With the coming dark,
Civil twilight, and the
Darkness after,
Our eyes accustomed to
Movement in the grass
That brings us to
Another border,
Where alfalfa, the coming
Rain soften the air enough
To breathe as the many
Teepee burners behind us
Flare in the night
As though signals
From a world not yet made—
And at the border
The coachman is waiting,
For each of us pays
For our sins in the manner
Of another's choosing—
The ghost that is always there.

RAIN LAST NIGHT, BUT NO SAINTS.

I'm writing this with blood
In the lugs of my boots,
Come up from the slaughtering swale.
No saints in the hunger and rot
Of our dreams. Look at your hands
Touching every dead thing
They have made. Oh, the quaking
Palms we want to trust,
Thrust toward us wanting
To stave off the knife
As wet grass dries in the sun
And behind us other voices pleading.

THE APPLE TREES ARE COLD TODAY.
A few leaves cup some night-rain
Out of the breeze that moves them.
Deer droppings glisten in weeds
Between faint tracks of coyotes.
The thistle has shriveled on its stem,
And I follow a line of geese
Above the house until they fade
Into the woodsmoke from the valley.

THE OVERCAST DIMMING, THE TORRENTIAL HUES

Of who we once were return—
You who stood there, face in your hands,
Such attitudes of grief before the real grief came.
For now, the blade will not strike you
And the voices are restless this morning,
Such things to tell you. I remember
Being lifted, borne aloft, and when
I returned your bright path faded
Into the dense and fragrant understory.
Here, frantic swarms the swallows kite through
In the growing shadow of the barn
As I shield the picture of your face
From the rains that hover.

THIN FLIES RISING FROM THE SNOW

And already there is grieving,
Starling interrogatives of the predawn.
Some dogs are barking and smoke
Of morning fattens into haze no gelding
Eats between the trailer-house clusters
Shining in the swale, and I think
Of what has happened, there,
In the simple past, where you too
Are waking like this, with your hand
Held out to a nothingness touching
The whorls as it passes by the window
Looking out on the only harvest I know.

I WITNESS THE LIGHT'S GRADATIONS ON THE UNCLAIMED FIELD,

Thinking of the violence that brings forth seeds,
That momentary lushness of blooms—how we embrace
The annihilation, the dying back to soil. In summer,
There are crows above us always. Maybe one hawk
Often. I think of the molecules that compose the field.
I think of the blood that surrounds us, how one strand
Of barbed wire can flay a man if it breaks just right.
Think of the farmer using his truck as a tensioner
Stringing up a wire, how quietly the unstapled wire
Coiled around him when it gave, and the truck in neutral
Towed him, in a reddening halo, into the cottonwoods
Below. Think what it feels like to come home
Without flesh, late in the cooling, pigeons
Not rising around you.

AFTER GREAT PATIENCE, A SMALL BIRD COMES.
In the mind's thin light, which is all
The presence we have of the eventual
World, the bird begins gently
To weave a nest
Of long dark strands
From your mother's hair.

I DREAM THE LIGHT MOVES A BLUE LAND.
Ice rots into river, a sudden loosening
Of the earth, wisps that are
My weather, raw winter-birds,
And on the southern aspects, the vestige
Of return: green sprig, hovering weed,
Harrow rusted in the field of mute.

MANY ARE THE VEHICLES

By which we are carried
To the perimeters of
Clarity, where the body
Tightens and winnows out
All but the yearning
To speak only a moment
In eternal tongue. There
Has been much rain.
The pasture is a river
With many horses in it
And I do not know where
You are, so I keep on
Ringing the warped bells
That sing, *Belong, belong.*

ISN'T THERE ALWAYS THAT FACE COMING INTO VIEW

That drags us forward into the damp night
Where a few pellets of sleet continue to fall
As we walk the slick road for hours, wondering
What it is that we've become?
And as those blue eyes plead for shelter,
Are we not left denying the mistakes,
The misadventures, the watching of the houses
As they, one after another, are involved
In flame, until nothing but ash remains
Of what was once our youth?
And that face taunting us with its beauty.
Don't our faces become infused with those
Who reside now only in the few moments
We carry with us? As we wander, do we not see
Hands reaching toward us from where
There is barely light? Hands that will cleanse us,
That will let us live again?

IT IS MORNING, AND TODAY IT WILL SNOW.

I'm standing in what light I can
Before the first flakes dampen against me,
The grass blades, the tall and leafless trees.
I do not know what the snow will give,
But every time I read your words I am
Broken open. If all the world is restraint
Then the dead are not wasted
But are granted the condition of tongues.
Here is the burn in the throat,
The constriction of the muscles around the lungs
That force our voices into the air.
Here, as wind tatters leaves on the ground,
Here, in the octave of the sweetest singing—
We, who have not written such songs.

THEN I CAME TO THE RIVER, SAT DOWN.
Traffic had thinned after the work rush,
The sky was marked with narrow clouds,
Air bitter from the asphalt plant
Further up the valley. The waters shushed
The stones of the levee, and from
The other shore kid-calls in their high tones
From the backs of houses on the bluff.
I moved my ear out of the wind,
And lights in the windows came on,
Families moved with their plates piled high
With slop. On the plateau behind the bluffs,
Reverberations of an announcer calling
The high school game, and suddenly
I remembered the pale birds
That enter our dreams, that we think
Nothing of, though it is their bloody task
To shred our each and every soul.

SOMETIMES I CAN PULL BEING VISIBLE. Sometimes it's just witch-talk and the songs of never-wills fuming the breeze, a luscious hovering that is no home, that is a fruitful demise at the threshold of the original door, as rain hunkers in, splaying its mood through the valley. I listen to the beasts sway their berths with salty frolic and wonder if the brain has forgotten its patterns of praise. How do we withstand when every day is *lily*? Fire ants are carcassing a bluebird, and the hour is in need of weeding, though the hand-planed singsong gods are made too bright and raw for us and the words we burn are impossible to carry.

SHALL WE SPEAK IN THE VOICE OF FIRE?

Sometimes it is tragedy that sustains us
But tell me, what do you do with the body
Even though we are made to be awkward,
Though we must embrace the annihilation
In the winterest light, though we sing
For the roughness that brings forth
Seeds and we make a lushness that we
Cannot be prepared for, little one,
Helpful ghost, most desolate chest,
What a burden we are to the living.

PUFFS OF DRY DIRT WHERE I SPRAIL A DARK LINE OF SPIT

Gritty with the blear of harvest waiting
For the morning trucks to haul our swaths of grain
From the upper field where the pale pine moths
Flutter the border trees where shade has vanished
And the water jugs are warming by the fence
And a few shirts drape out to dry reeking of yesterday
As the combines tick adding their heat
To the moment and across the road round bales
Blanch and waver as I wipe the cuff of my leather glove
Where sweat bleeds through it as I grind tobacco
Between my teeth and spit again and glance
The far-off haze as the soils absorb the violence
And a cluster of starlings launch from the stubble
Into the smoking August air.

AS IF WE ARE PART OF THE READYING,
The coagulants out of some dream
In the ruptured order of snow,
The chaos terrains in the myopic smear
Of a voided land through which
Wind devolves, the momentary
Attitude of form, the wordless furnace
Churning in the dark, all tensile
And heave, like the manic resolutions
Of the lost: if I'm found: if they come,
Like the metered articulations
Of the deepening constellations,
Whatever grace I contain, obtain
Remains always in the beyond,
Out there, in what is granted now
And now is taken.

AS THE MOON DUMPS ITS PALE INK

Across the dark page of the world
I listen for the little god
That flies out before us
Warning the way of our muffled arriving,
For we have wandered far
And even now there is no home
To return to though we stand
On the prow of a ship come to port
Where everyone has gathered to greet us
And sob into our arms once more.

CHLOROPHYLL MORNING,

Death-scent of lilac
Tipping out the rain,
And on the field
A fallow calm falls
Leaving the soil
To its feraling.
White blossoms of
Ninebark shimmy
Where birds plush
And hold hard to trees
As wind expresses
Fricatives through
The beetled pine—
The air gets dim,
As day-plants
Withhold their blooms
From the transit of Venus,
As rain slurries down
In the marking off
Of time, as rain
Gathers in the eye
Of a blackbird.

AT WHAT POINT DO WE STOP ASKING

To be *made*? The music ends,
The musician misremembers
And nature must be granted its way
As it devours the cruel
And the just evenly.
There was a belief, somewhere.
A belief, some faith, a mother standing by
Pistol in her hand. Where can we go
If what is laid before us
Belongs to someone else?
In this, the day resides
And within it the moments we cannot influence
As light accrues then unclasps itself
As I stand again in a field that once
Belonged to me, calming my son
By whispering to his small form
The stories of what has come to pass,
Who did what to whom, and why.

LINE OF GEESE DRAWING SOUTH,

Mist in retrograde, 6 am, zero sleep—
Who will guide me now
Through slim days of winterhood,
The soft whumping of lighter fluid
Charging the wood with flame—
I do not want to waste the light,
The white cloud above you—
Listen, there's bound to be
A few nails in your heart—
There's bound to be some missing.
If we believe in the epicenter,
How many years does it take
To embrace the gutted and the shorn?
This is what we did: lived for a while,
Were happy, and here does memory sit
Holding us to each other,
That binds us and bids us
To place our bodies
On the white coals of time.

IN A WINTER WOOD WE HEAR IT,
The child's voice that visits us
After such a life as this—
How soft, yet how clear the words
Though surely the child grew
As you did, and suffered the world
And now, after so many silent years
The voice speaks clear, saying words
That were said once before,
And as the journey slows
You put your white head in your hands
And kneel to the compacted snow
As the lights of the far town deepen.

ALL MORNING I'VE WATCHED THE VOLE

Kitter through the grass
From the hole in the foundation
To the crack in the cinder block
Pump house, pausing here and there,
Her body full of other bodies.
Just now I saw the pale flash
Of her belly as she turned, looked back
And wedged herself into safety.
The sky is warming the windowpane,
My clean work shirt,
The Goodwill cassette player
Clicking off at the end of Górecki,
As I sit on the bench, rubbing
The stock of my .410 slowly.

YOU KNOW WHAT THE PRICE IS NOW.
Standing in the darkening rain
Watching the yellow light
Of a small house beneath some pine.
The ghost-child is reaching
For your hand, pale patches
Of breath smearing the air,
Wool coat heavy as a tragedy
That brings us here, this hand
In your hand, the furnace
Of our cruel days, and to know
The strands that keep us here
Are fraying, and that we have
No place to harbor through—
The heft of the ghost
When we lift it, its alien heart
Beating in time to ours.

ACKNOWLEDGMENTS

The author would like to thank Allen Braden, Kim Burwick, and Rebecca Gayle Howell for their critical attention to this work.

And Shawna Overman (1967-2010), for early tendernesses.

RECENT TITLES FROM ALICE JAMES BOOKS

Light Me Down: The New & Collected Poems of Jean Valentine, Jean Valentine

Song of My Softening, Omotara James

Theophanies, Sarah Ghazal Ali

Orders of Service, Willie Lee Kinard III

The Dead Peasant's Handbook, Brian Turner

The Goodbye World Poem, Brian Turner

The Wild Delight of Wild Things, Brian Turner

I Am the Most Dangerous Thing, Candace Williams

Burning Like Her Own Planet, Vandana Khanna

Standing in the Forest of Being Alive, Katie Farris

Feast, Ina Cariño

Decade of the Brain: Poems, Janine Joseph

American Treasure, Jill McDonough

We Borrowed Gentleness, J. Estanislao Lopez

Brother Sleep, Aldo Amparán

Sugar Work, Katie Marya

Museum of Objects Burned by the Souls in Purgatory, Jeffrey Thomson

Constellation Route, Matthew Olzmann

How to Not Be Afraid of Everything, Jane Wong

Brocken Spectre, Jacques J. Rancourt

No Ruined Stone, Shara McCallum

The Vault, Andrés Cerpa

White Campion, Donald Revell

Last Days, Tamiko Beyer

If This Is the Age We End Discovery, Rosebud Ben-Oni

Pretty Tripwire, Alessandra Lynch

Inheritance, Taylor Johnson

The Voice of Sheila Chandra, Kazim Ali

Alice James Books is committed to publishing books that matter. The press was founded in 1973 in Boston, Massachusetts to give women access to publishing. As a cooperative, authors performed the day-to-day undertakings of the press. The press continues to expand and grow from its formative roots, guided by its founding values of access, excellence, inclusivity, and collaboration in publishing. Its mission is to publish books that matter and preserve a place of belonging for poets who inspire us. AJB seeks to broaden our collective interpretation of what constitutes the American poetic voice and is dedicated to helping its artists achieve purposeful engagement with broad audiences and communities nationwide. The press was named for Alice James, sister to William and Henry, whose extraordinary gift for writing went unrecognized during her lifetime.

Designed by Kenji Liu

Printed by Sheridan Saline